T0342951

CANBERRA

CANBERRA
THE BUSH CAPITAL

NEW HOLLAND

INTRODUCTION

Canberra, Australia's capital, is a city unique in Australia, and therefore the world.

Nicknamed the 'Bush Capital', it is classed as one of the most liveable cities in Australia for it's fresh air, cycleways and rarely congested traffic. Well-planned, it features modern architecture amongst abundant bushland. Cold in the winter, with nights often below zero, and hot and dry in summer.

Home to the Australian Parliament House, Canberra is also known for its many social and cultural institutions, such as the Australian War Memorial focusing on the military history of Australia; the Australian Institute of Sport; The Australian National University, ranked 30th in the world by QS; Questacon; and the National Gallery of Australia showcasing thousands of works of art from Australia and around the world.

The National Museum of Australia has an incredible collection of stories of Australia through their exhibitions and guided tours as well as showcasing the natural world of objects and ideas. The National Library of Australia holds the past and present of Australia in publications, maps and rare works that are collected and preserved.

The man-made Lake Burley Griffin is the heart of the city and most days you will find people taking walks, cycling or running around its lush surroundings of peace and beauty. The Australian National Botanic Gardens showcases the country's unique flora and attracts visitors all year round.

The Canberra food scene is busy with markets and festivals throughout the year showcasing good produce of everything Canberra has to offer with beer breweries and vineyards to visit, as well as award-winning restaurants.

View from Mount Ainslie. In the centre is the Australian War Memorial and Anzac Parade, then across Lake Burley Griffin is Old Parliament House (now the Museum of Australian Democracy) and Parliament House. To the right is the City Centre, known by locals as Civic.

Compare this photo with the original architectural vision of Canberra on the following spread.

COMMONWEALTH
OF AUSTRALIA
FEDERAL CAPITAL
COMPETITION

VIEW FROM
SVMMIT OF
MOVNT AINSLIE

Walter Burleigh Griffin's original vision of Canberra. Painting by Marion Mahony.

THE CENTRE
OF CANBERRA

Civic centre

View of the city looking north

Sydney building

Glebe Park

21

Apartments and commercial buildings at Parkes Way

Gorman House Arts Centre

The Civic Square in Canberra featuring Canberra Museum and Gallery, Canberra Theatre Centre, and the famous 'Ethos' statue

City centre

The Shine Dome, the headquarters of the Australian Academy of Science

ANU John Curtin School of Medical Research

ANU campus

LAKE BURLEY GRIFFIN

Canberra Balloon Spectacular

Captain Cook Memorial Globe

Commonwealth Avenue Bridge viewed from the National Capital Exhibition Centre

Queen Elizabeth Terrace

Commonwealth Place

Lake Burley Griffin and the National Museum of Australia

Commonwealth Bridge over Lake Burley Griffin

49

National Museum of Australia and Canberra Balloon Spectacular

53

Telstra Tower on Black Mountain

Kingston Foreshore

Captain Cook Memorial Jet

National Carillon

National Carillon

Canberra Balloon Spectacular on Lake Burley Griffin

THE SEAT OF
GOVERNMENT

Parliament House with Old Parliament House in the foreground. Questacon at right.

Parliament House

The Senate chambers

Main foyer of Australian Parliament House

Hallway of the Parliament House with prime minister portraits

National Film and Sound Archive of Australia (NFSA)

Russell Offices, administrative headquarters of the Australian Defence Forces featuring the Australian–American Memorial

Royal Military College, Duntroon parade ground

John Gorton Building

The Lodge, the officail prime minister's residence, is rarely open to the public

Government House, official residence of the Governor-General

Royal Thai Embassy, one of the many foreign embassies in Canberra

Aboriginal Tent Embassy in Canberra Parliamentary Zone

MUSEUMS AND CULTURE

Old Parliament House, now the Museum of Australian Democracy

National Gallery of Australia

Neil Dawson's Diamonds

James Turrell's 'Within without' Skyspace

High Court of Australia

MAIN READING ROOM

National Library of Australia foyer

National Library with Questacon behind,and Treasury.
On the right, West Block on Constitution Avenue and Parliament House.

Albert Hall

National Archives of Australia

Australian War Memorial

Dome at the Australian War Memorial

"G for George" aircraft in the Anzac Hall of Australian War Memorial

The Flanders poppy is the symbol of Remembrance Day, marking the Armistice of 11 November 1918, at the Australian War Memorial

Simpson and his Donkey
statue in the sculpture
garden of the Australian War
Memorial

Survivors statue commemorating the sacrifice of Australian merchant seamen

Centurion tank outside the Australian War Memorial.

The War Dog Memorial at the Australian War Memorial

National Museum of Australia

national museum of australia

Muttaburrasaurus

149

AIS | visitor cent

An Olympic Training Centre
recognised by the
Australian Olympic Committee

Questacon – The National Science and Technology Centre

Questacon during the Enlighten Festival

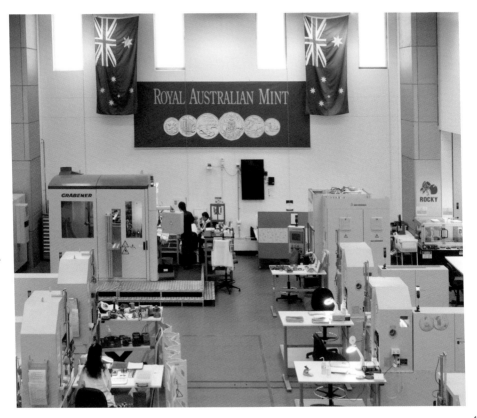

Royal Australian Mint, Deakin

SUBURBAN CANBERRA

Tuggeranong

Canberra suburbs

Big Splash Waterpark, Macquarie

Kingston Foreshore

Canberra Glassworks

Manuka Village

Manuka Pool built in 1930

St John's Anglican Church, Reid

St Christopher's Cathedral, Manuka/Forrest

Old Canberra Brickworks, Yarralumla

Canberra Nara Peace Park, Yarralumla

Mercure Canberra, Braddon

Old Bus Depot Markets, Kingston

GIO Stadium Canberra, Bruce

TRANSPORT

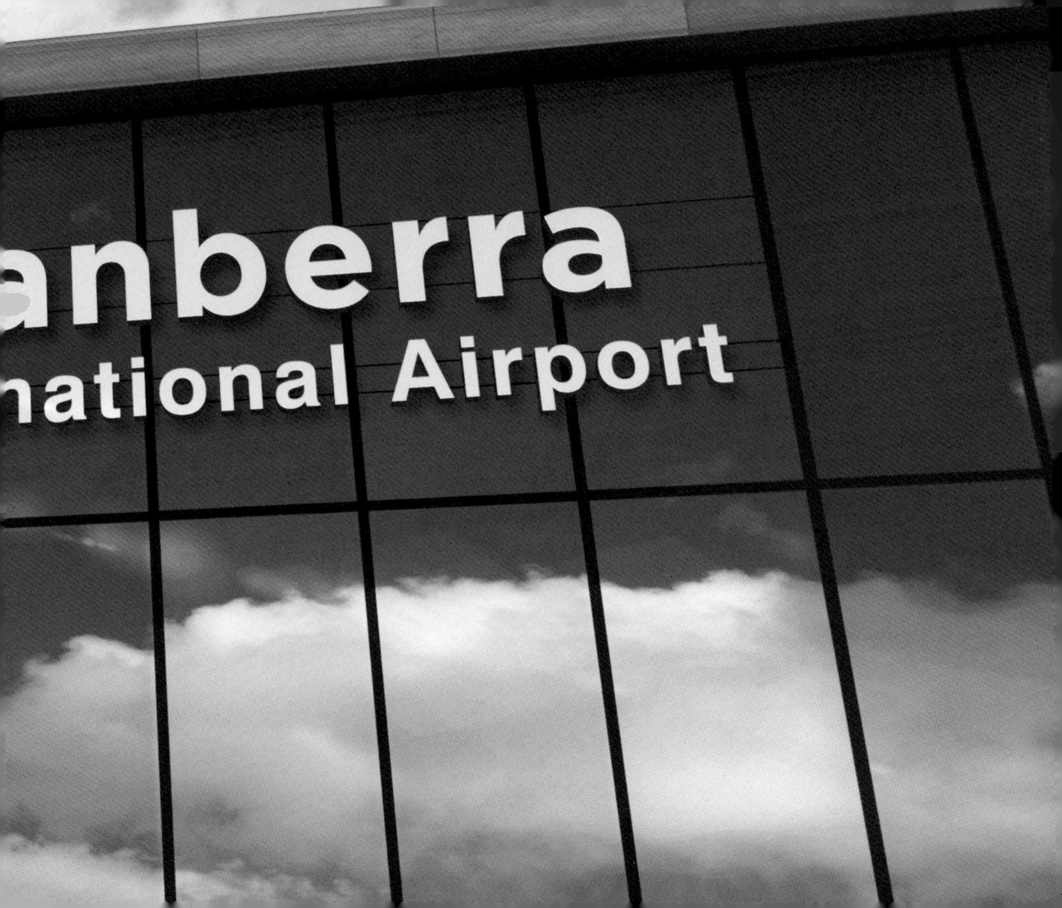
anberra
national Airport

Alinga Street light rail stop affected by bushfire smoke

Canberra Metro light rail

ACTION bus in Civic

Iconic Canberra bus stop

Traffic on Commonwealth Avenue

Summernats

CANBERRA REGION

Red Rock Gorge from Kambah Pool Reserve

Canberra Deep Space Communication Complex, Tidbinbilla

Tidbinbilla

Now closed Mount Stromlo Café and Visitor Centre

National Dinosaur Museum, Nicholls

Cotter Dam provides a part
of Canbeerra's water supply.

Lanyon Homestead, Tharwa

National Arboretum Canberra at dawn viewed from lookout at Dairy Farmers Hill

National Arboretum Canberra with the
Margaret Whitlam Pavilion in foreground

National Arboretum Canberra

National Arboretum Canberra Village Centre

Playground at the National Arboretum Canberra

Australian National Botanic Gardens

Crocodile at National Zoo & Aquarium, Yarralumla

Peacock at National Zoo & Aquarium, Yarralumla

Giraffe at National Zoo & Aquarium

Meerkats at National Zoo & Aquarium

Kangaroos

Snow on the Brindabella Range, NSW, contributes to Canberra's cold winter

First published in 2024 by New Holland Publishers
Sydney

Level 1, 178 Fox Valley Road, Wahroonga, NSW 2076, Australia

newhollandpublishers.com

A record of this book is held at the National Library of Australia.

ISBN 9781760797713

Managing Director: Fiona Schultz
General Manager/Publisher: Olga Dementiev
Designer: Andrew Davies
Production Director: Arlene Gippert
Printed in China

10 9 8 7 6 5 4 3 2 1

Keep up with New Holland Publishers:
 NewHollandPublishers
 @newhollandpublishers